Victorian Spot Illustrations, Alphabets and Ornaments
from Porret's Type Catalog

Edited by
Carol Belanger Grafton

DOVER PUBLICATIONS, INC.
NEW YORK

Copyright © 1982 by Dover Publications, Inc.
All rights reserved under Pan American and International Copyright Conventions.

Published in Canada by General Publishing Company, Ltd., 30 Lesmill Road, Don Mills, Toronto, Ontario.
Published in the United Kingdom by Constable and Company, Ltd., 10 Orange Street, London WC2H 7EG.

Victorian Spot Illustrations, Alphabets and Ornaments from Porret's Type Catalog is a new work, first published by Dover Publications, Inc., in 1982.

DOVER *Pictorial Archive* SERIES

Manufactured in the United States of America
Dover Publications, Inc.
31 East 2nd Street
Mineola, N.Y. 11501

Library of Congress Cataloging in Publication Data
Main entry under title:

Victorian spot illustrations, alphabets, and ornaments from Porret's type catalog.

1. Wood-engraving, Victorian — France — Themes, motives. 2. Wood-engraving, French — Themes, motives. 3. Porret, Henri Désiré. Illustrations typographiques. I. Grafton, Carol Belanger. II. Porret, Henri Désiré. Illustrations typographiques. III. Title.
NE1092.V5   769.5   81-17360
ISBN 0-486-24271-4   AACR2

Contents

Publisher's Note

Artists and designers desiring a copyright-free illustration or ornament need look no further than this excellent selection of nineteenth-century pictorial materials. Here are decorative alphabets, allegorical figures, people, animals, flowers, fruits, costumes, ornaments, and more—all printed on high-quality stock to insure a superior image when used as camera-ready art.

This Dover publication has been derived from Henri-Désiré Porret's *Illustrations Typographiques,* a two-volume work published in Paris between 1838 and 1842. Porret, who worked for the French royal printing establishment, made his engravings on wood, the principal medium during the Romantic period for the reproduction of illustrations in books and periodicals. In the hands of such excellent practitioners as Porret, wood engraving could achieve artistic expression of great distinction. Porret's intention was identical to ours: to provide an interesting miscellany of illustrations for reproduction—what is today referred to as a "swipe file." There is an important historical and technological distinction: Porret sold actual engravings, which were identified by number and priced in the catalog; the illustrations in this Dover volume are primarily intended for use in offset reproduction.

The selection from Porret by Carol Belanger Grafton has been made with an eye toward retaining Porret's finest work and to provide those illustrations that will best serve the needs of today's artists and designers.

Aigle (eagle)

Butor (bittern)

Chien (dog)

Dromadaire (dromedary)

Éléphant (elephant)

Fouine (marten)

Grenouille (frog)

Hibou (owl)

Ibis (ibis)

Jabira (jabiru)

Kanguroo (kangaroo)

Lyre (lyrebird)

Mouton (sheep)

Nandou (rhea)

Ours (bear)

Panthère (panther)

Quereivo

Renard (fox)

Singe (monkey)

Tortue (tortoise)

Urdon (porcupine)

Vache (cow)

White-Patoroo

Xandarus

Yapock (water opossum)

Zébu (zebu)

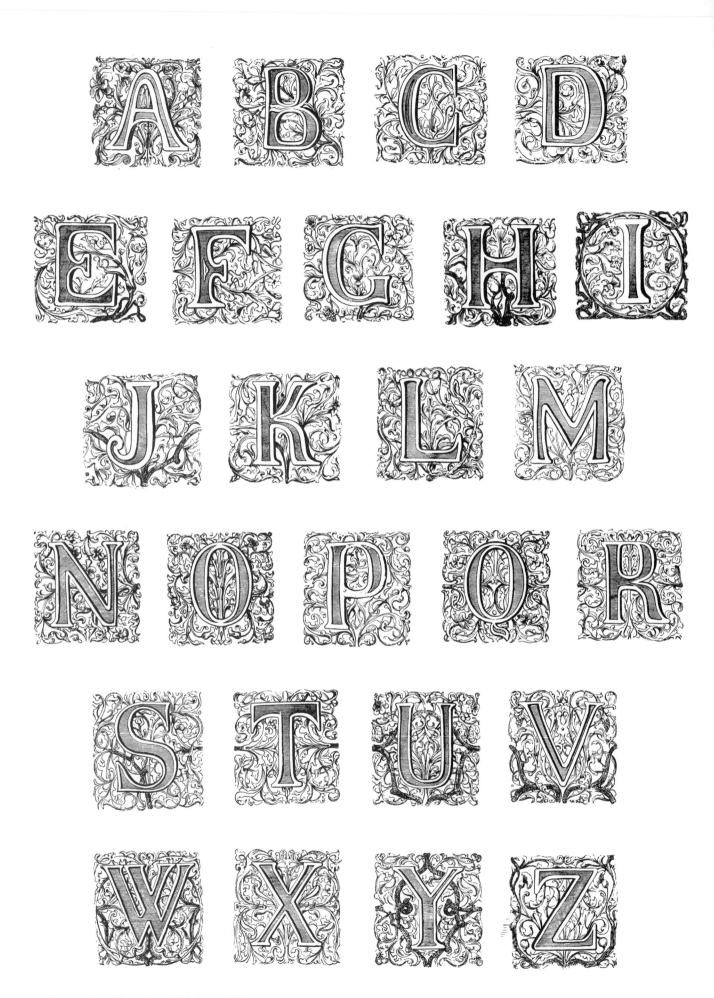

Victorian Spot Illustrations, Alphabets and Ornaments

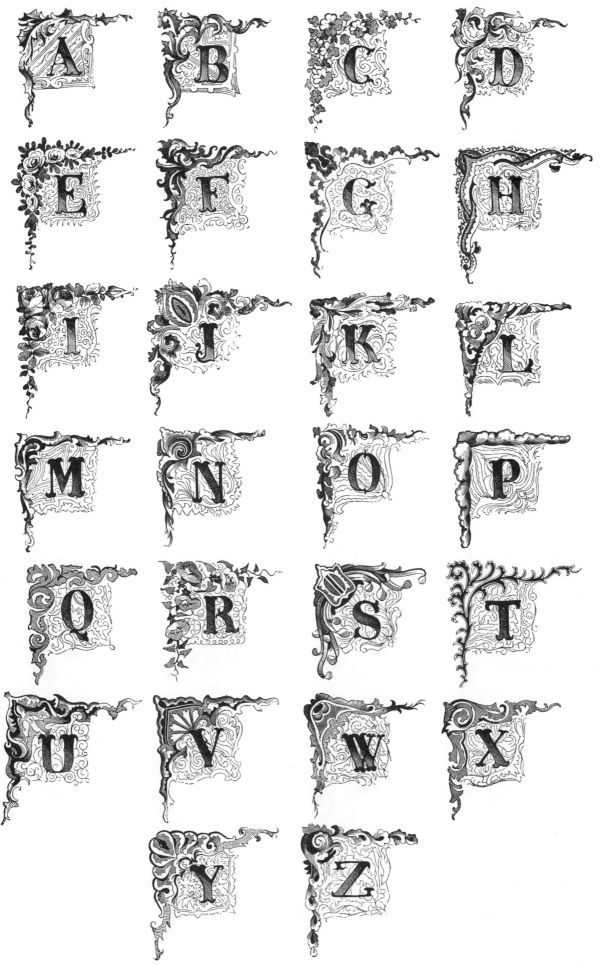

Amarante (love-lies-bleeding)

Blé de Turquie (maize)

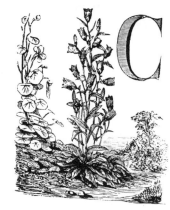

Campanule (bellflower)

Dysacus

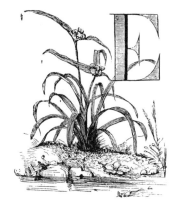

Ephémère (spiderwort)

Fraise (strawberry)

Geranium (geranium)

Hortensia (hortensia)

Iris (iris)

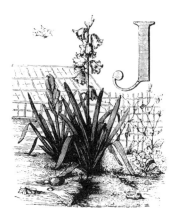

Jacynthe (hyacinth)

Ketsoura

Liseron (bindweed)

Mauve (mallow)

Narcisse (narcissus)

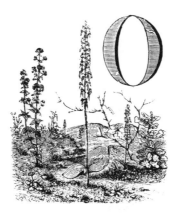

Ophryse (orchis)

Pavot (poppy)

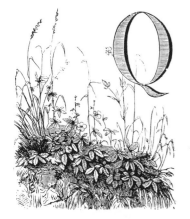

Quintefeuille (cinquefoil)

Rose trémière (hollyhock)

Sceau de Salomon (Solomon's seal)

Trèfle (clover)

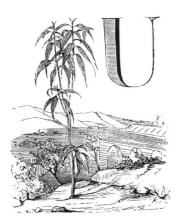

Urtica (nettle)

Violette (violet)

Vigne et Volubilis (grapes and convolvulus)

Xantorba

Yuca (yucca)

Zalia

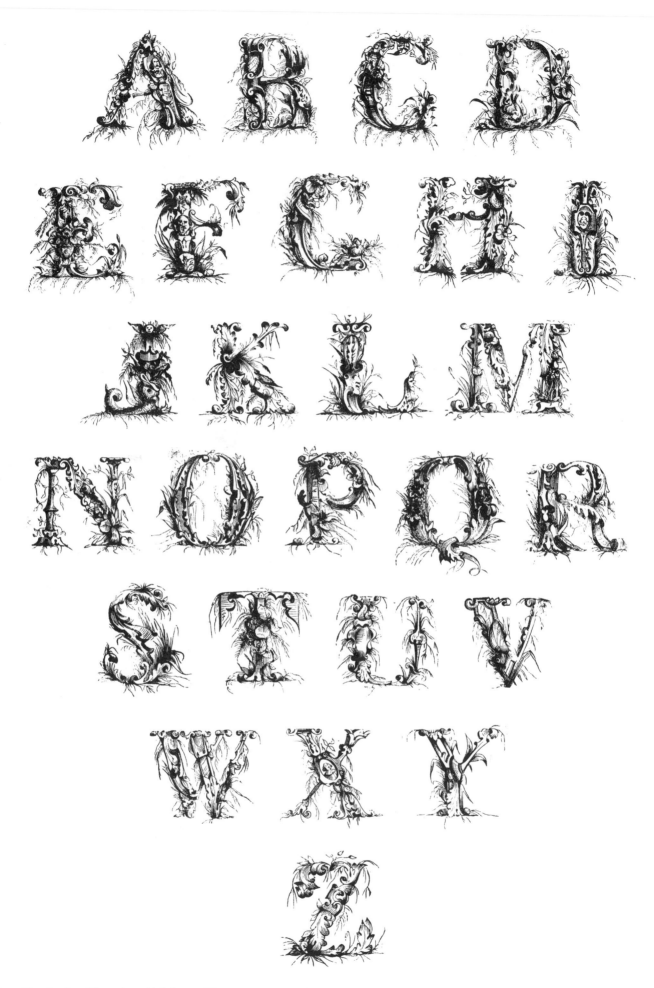

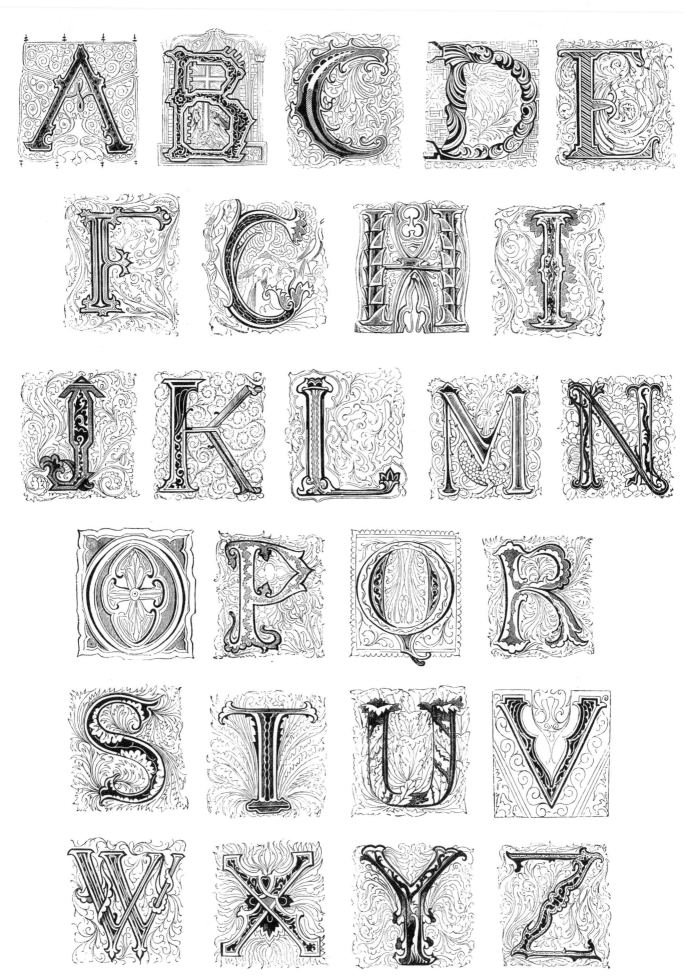

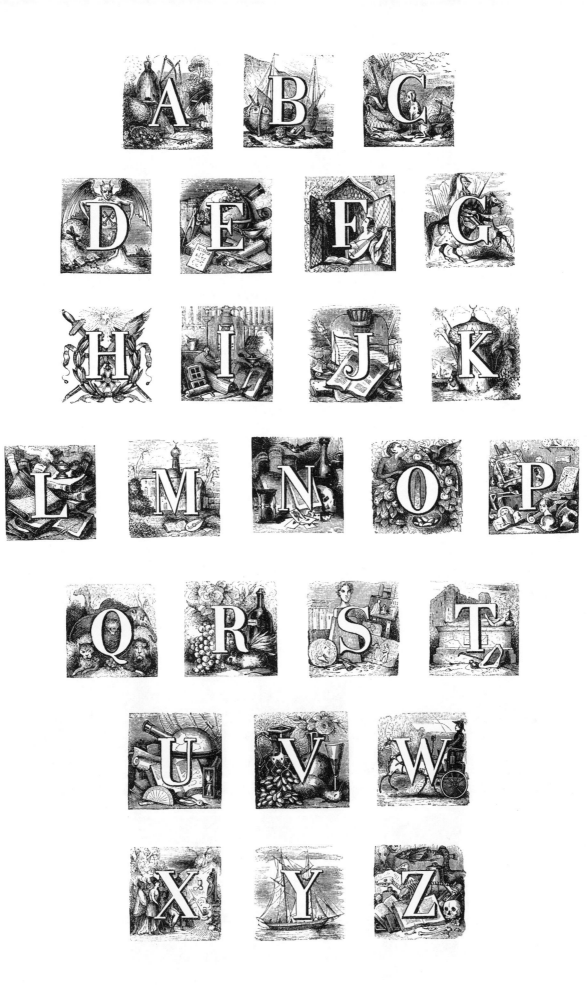

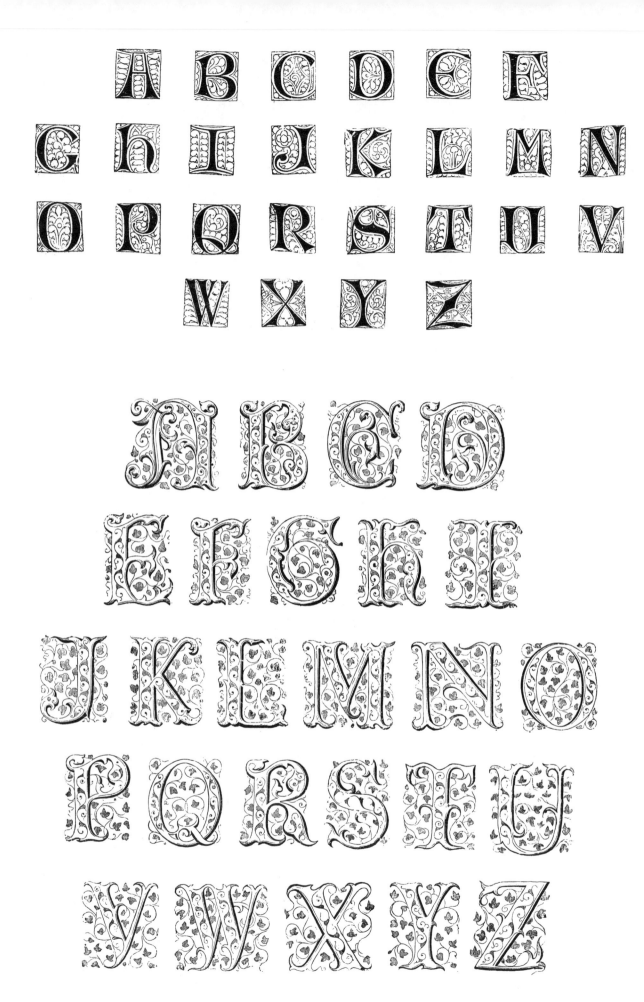

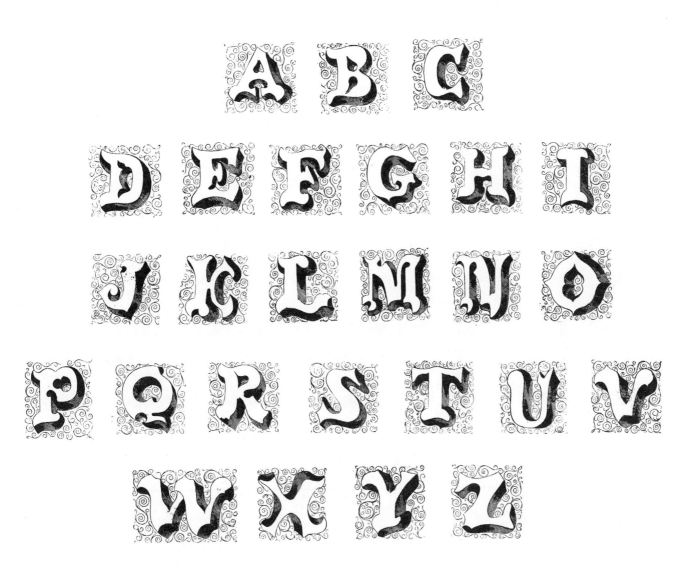

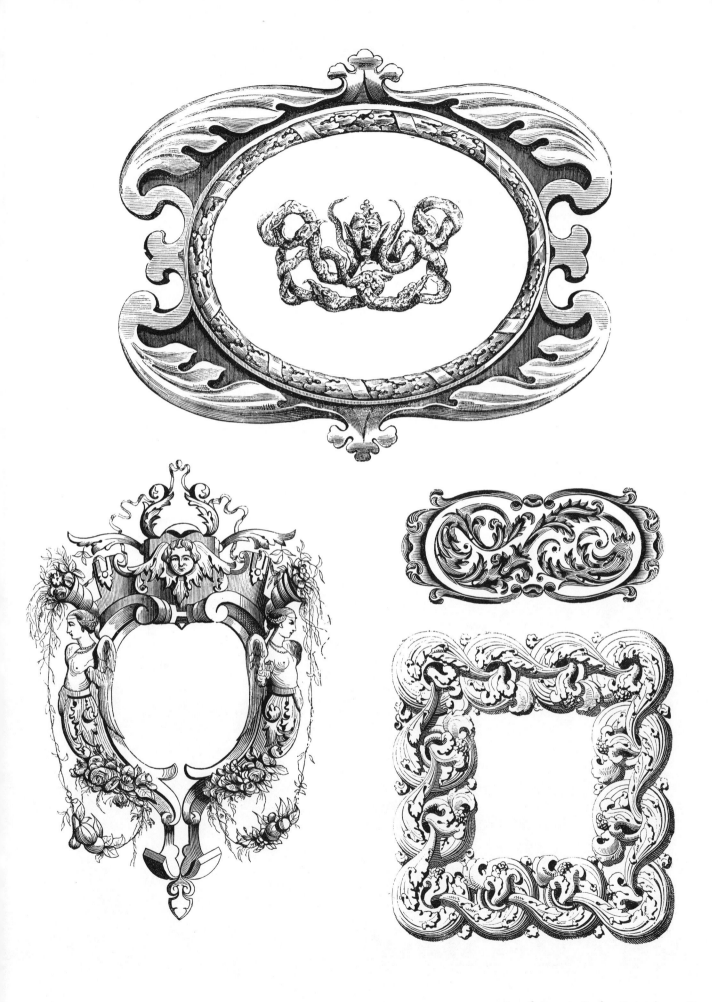

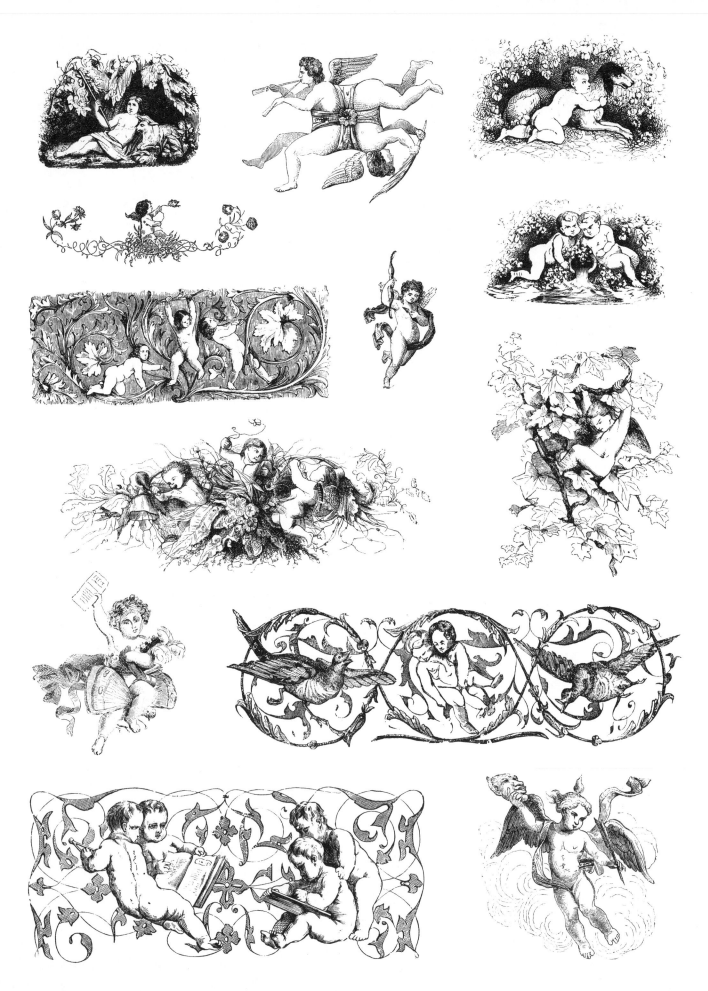

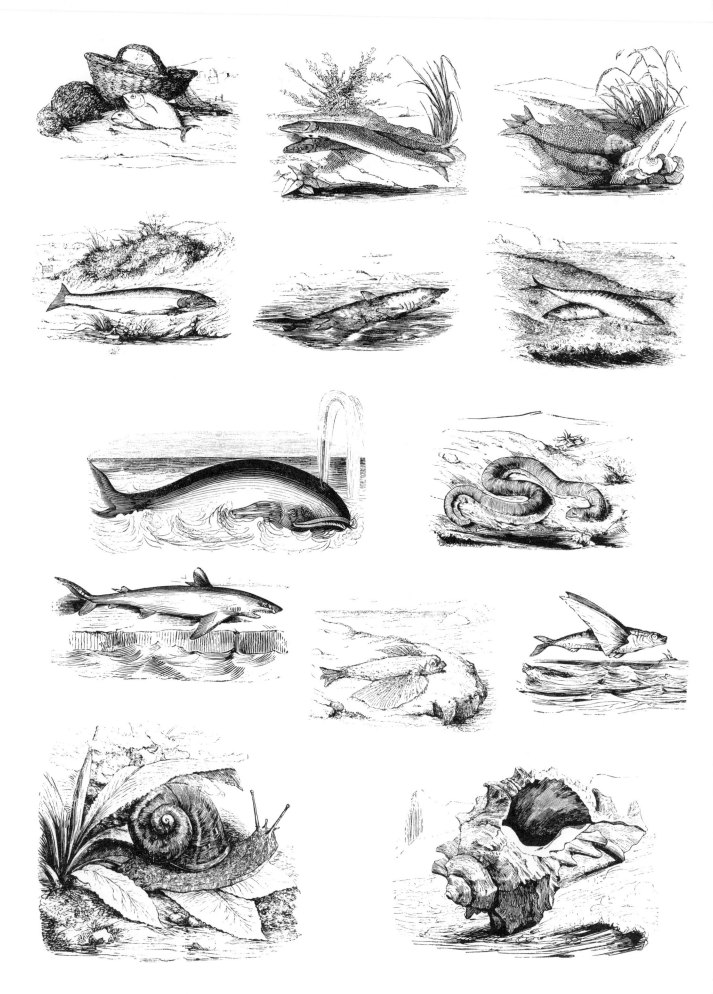

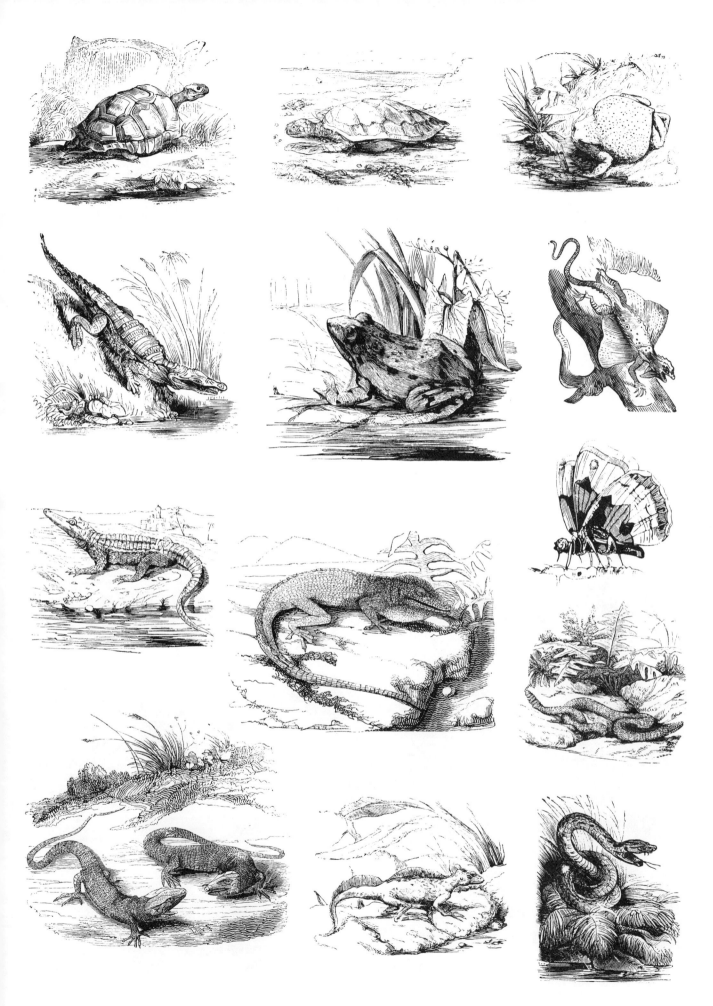

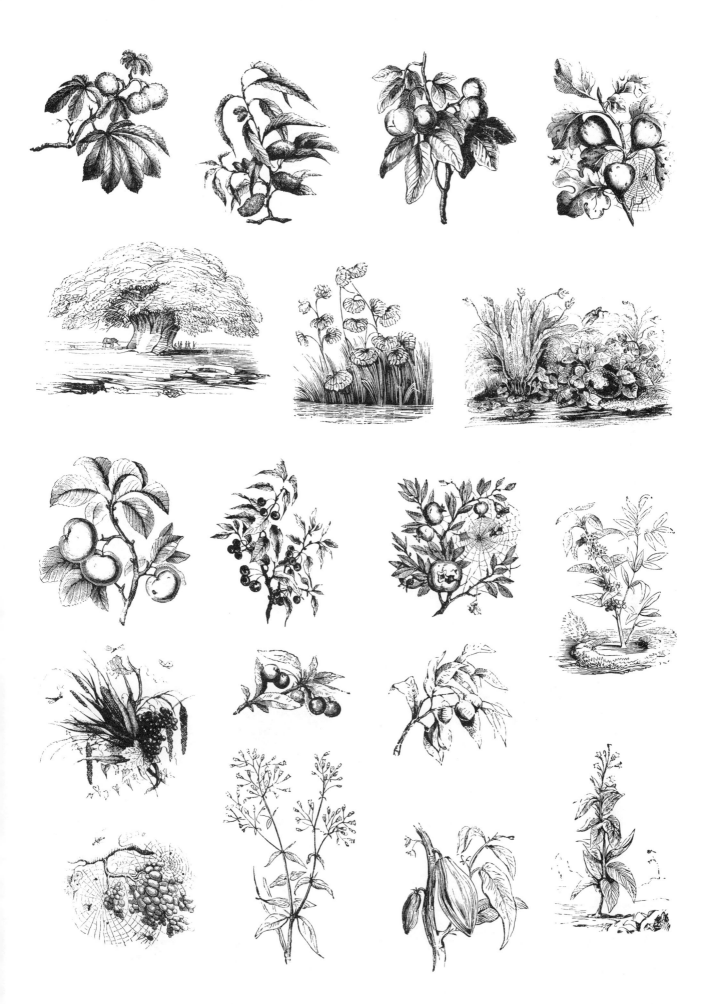

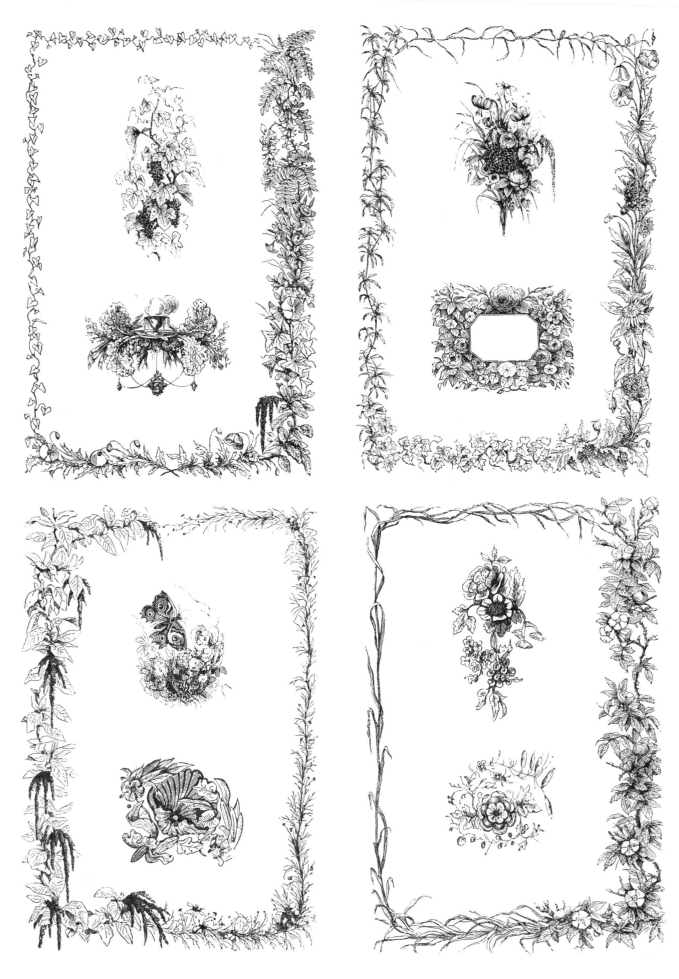

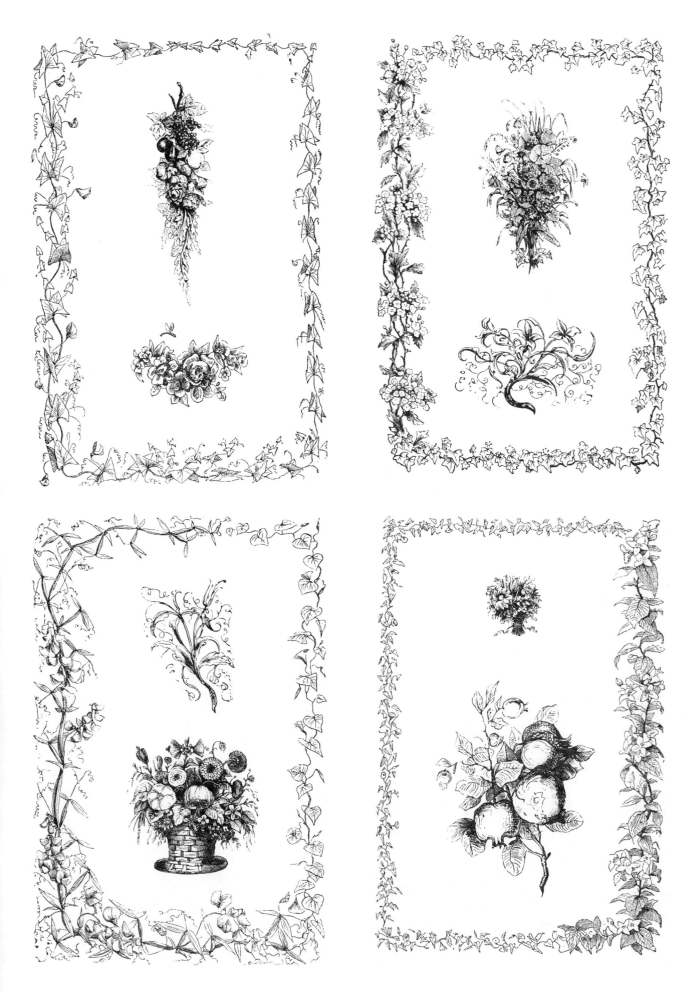